French Short Stories for Beginners
Book 1

Over 100 Dialogues and Daily Used Phrases to Learn French in Your Car. Have Fun & Grow Your Vocabulary, with Crazy Effective Language Learning Lessons

LEARN LIKE A NATIVE
www.LearnLikeNatives.com

TABLE OF CONTENT

INTRODUCTION

Before we dive into some French, I want to congratulate you, whether you're just beginning, continuing, or resuming your language learning journey. Here at Learn Like a Native, we understand the determination it takes to pick up a new language and after reading this book, you'll be another step closer to achieving your language goals. As a thank you for learning with us, we are giving you free access to our 'Speak Like a Native' eBook. It's packed full of practical advice and insider tips on how to make language learning quick, easy, and most importantly, enjoyable. Head over to LearnLikeNatives.com to access your free guide and peruse our huge selection of language learning resources.

Learning a new language is a bit like cooking—you need several different ingredients and the right technique, but the end result is sure to be delicious. We created this book of short stories for learning French because language is alive. Language is about the senses—hearing, tasting the words on your tongue, and touching another culture up close. Learning a language in a classroom is a fine place to start, but it's not a complete introduction to a language.

In this book, you'll find a language come to life. These short stories are miniature immersions into the French language, at a level that is perfect for beginners. This book is not a lecture on grammar. It's not an endless vocabulary list. This book is the closest you can come to a language immersion without leaving the country. In the stories within, you will see people speaking to each other, going through daily life situations, and using the most common, helpful words and phrases in language.

You are holding the key to bringing your French studies to life.

Made for Beginners

We made this book with beginners in mind. You'll find that the language is simple, but not boring. Most of the book is in the present tense, so you will be able to focus on dialogues, root verbs, and understand and find patterns in subject-verb agreement.

This is not "just" a translated book. While reading novels and short stories translated into French is a wonderful thing, beginners (and even novices) often run into difficulty. Literary licenses and complex sentence structure can make reading in your second language truly difficult—not to mention BORING. That's why French Short Stories for Beginners is the perfect book to pick up. The stories are simple, but not infantile. They were not written for children, but the language is simple so that beginners can pick it up.

The Benefits of Learning a Second Language

If you have picked up this book, it's likely that you are already aware of the many benefits of learning a second language. Besides just being fun, knowing more than one language opens up a whole new world to you. You will be able to communicate with a much larger chunk of the world. Opportunities in the workforce will open up, and maybe even your day-to-day work will be improved. Improved communication can also help you expand your business. And from a neurological perspective, learning a second language is like taking your daily vitamins and eating well, for your brain!

How To Use The Book

The chapters of this book all follow the same structure:

- A short story with several dialogs
- A summary in French
- A list of important words and phrases and their English translation
- Questions to test your understanding
- Answers to check if you were right
- The English translation of the story to clear every doubt

You may use this book however is comfortable for you, but we have a few recommendations for getting the most out of the experience. Try these tips and if they work for you, you can use them on every chapter throughout the book.

1) Start by reading the story all the way through. Don't stop or get hung up on any particular words or phrases. See how much of the plot you can understand in this way. We think you'll get a lot more of it than you may expect, but it is completely normal not to understand everything in the story. You are learning a new language, and that takes time.

2) Read the summary in French. See if it matches what you have understood of the plot.

3) Read the story through again, slower this time. See if you can pick up the meaning of any words or phrases you don't understand by using context clues and the information from the summary.

4) Test yourself! Try to answer the five comprehension questions that come at the end of each story. Write your answers

down, and then check them against the answer key. How did you do? If you didn't get them all, no worries!

5) Look over the vocabulary list that accompanies the chapter. Are any of these the words you did not understand? Did you already know the meaning of some of them from your reading?

6) Now go through the story once more. Pay attention this time to the words and phrases you haven't understand. If you'd like, take the time to look them up to expand your meaning of the story. Every time you read over the story, you'll understand more and more.

7) Move on to the next chapter when you are ready.

Read and Listen

The audio version is the best way to experience this book, as you will hear a native French speaker tell you each story. You will become accustomed to their accent as you listen along, a huge plus for when you want to apply your new language skills in the real world.

If this has ignited your language learning passion and you are keen to find out what other resources are available, go to **LearnLikeNatives.com**, where you can access our vast range of free learning materials. Don't know where to begin? An excellent place to start is our 'Speak Like a Native' free eBook, full of practical advice and insider tips on how to make language learning quick, easy, and most importantly, enjoyable.

And remember, small steps add up to great advancements! No moment is better to begin learning than the present.

FREE BOOK!

Get the *FREE BOOK* that reveals the secrets path to learn any language fast, and without leaving your country.

Discover:

- The **language 5 golden rules** to master languages at will

- Proven **mind training techniques** to revolutionize your learning

- A complete step-by-step guide to **conquering any language**

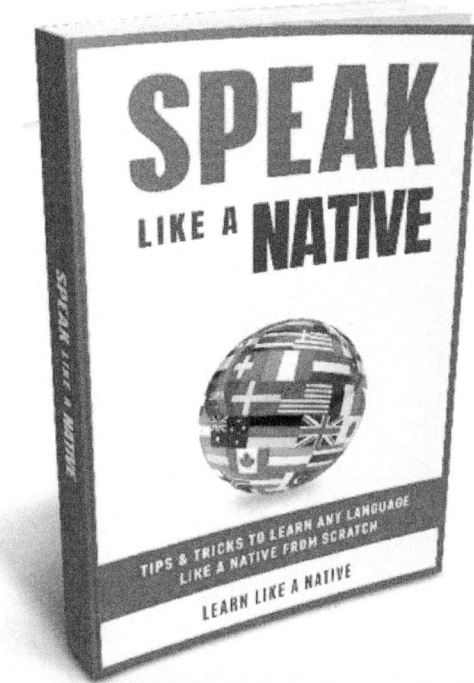

CHAPTER 1
The Mysterious Package / Greetings

La sonnette sonne.

Andrew court vers la porte de l'appartement. Personne ne sonne jamais le samedi matin. Andrew a hâte de voir qui est à la porte. Il ouvre la porte.

« **Bonjour**, petit garçon, dit un livreur. » L'homme est vêtu d'un uniforme brun et porte une boîte marron.

« **Bonjour, monsieur** », dit Andrew.

« J'ai un colis », dit le livreur. « Il est écrit 10, Grande Rue. »

« Nous sommes au 10, Grande Rue », dit Andrew.

« Le colis n'a pas de nom, dit le livreur. Il n'a pas non plus de numéro d'appartement. »

« Comme c'est étrange », dit Andrew.

«Pouvez-vous le donner à la bonne personne?», demande l'homme.

« Je peux essayer », dit Andrew. Il n'a que dix ans, mais il se sent important.

« **Merci beaucoup** », dit le livreur. Il part. Andrew ramène la boite chez lui. Il la fixe. Elle a à peu près la taille d'une boîte à chaussures. Il n'y a pas de nom de destinataire, seulement 10, Grande Rue.

Andrew ouvre la boîte en carton. Il a besoin de savoir ce qu'il y a à l'intérieur pour trouver le propriétaire. Il y a une petite boîte en bois à l'intérieur de la boîte en carton. Andrew ouvre la boîte en bois. À l'intérieur de la boîte se trouvent 10 paires de lunettes différentes. Elles sont de couleurs différentes : roses et rouges, à pois verts, noires et blanches. Les formes aussi sont différentes : rondes, carrées et rectangulaires.

Il ferme la boîte et met ses chaussures.

« **Au revoir** maman! Je reviens tout de suite », crie-t-il.

Andrew frappe à la porte en face de chez lui. Elle s'ouvre. Une très vieille dame sourit à Andrew et à la boîte.

« **Bonjour**, Mme Smith. » dit Andrew.

«**Comment vas-tu**?» demande la vieille dame.

« **Très bien, merci! Et vous?** », dit Andrew.

«Qu'est-ce que tu as là?» demande la vieille dame.

« **Madame**, c'est un paquet. Il appartient à quelqu'un dans cet immeuble, mais je ne sais pas à qui, dit Andrew.

« Ce n'est pas pour moi », dit la vieille dame. « Impossible! »

« Oh, ok », dit Andrew, déçu. La vieille dame porte des lunettes. Il pense que ces lunettes lui iraient bien. Il se retourne pour partir.

« Reviens plus tard », lui crie la vieille dame. « Je fais des biscuits et il y en a pour toi et ta famille. »

Andrew monte les escaliers. Son immeuble compte trois étages. Il est ami avec presque tout le monde dans l'immeuble. Cependant, il y a une nouvelle famille dans l'appartement du deuxième étage. Andrew ne les connaît pas. Il est intimidé, mais il sonne. Un homme brun ouvre la porte. Il sourit.

«**Salut!**» dit l'homme.

« Bonjour, dit Andrew. Je vis en bas. **Je m'appelle** Andrew. »

« **C'est un plaisir de faire ta connaissance**, Andrew », dit l'homme. « Nous sommes nouveaux dans l'immeuble. Je suis M. Jones. »

« **Moi aussi, je suis heureux de vous rencontrer** », dit Andrew. « Ce colis appartient à quelqu'un dans cet immeuble. Est-ce votre colis? »

«Impossible!» dit l'homme. «Ma famille et moi venons d'emménager ici. Personne ne connaît notre adresse.»

« D'accord », dit Andrew. « Ravi de vous rencontrer alors ». La porte se ferme. Un autre non. Il ne reste que deux appartements à essayer. Dans l'appartement suivant, il y a une famille. La fille fréquente la même école qu'Andrew. Elle a un an de plus qu'Andrew. Elle s'appelle Diana.

Andrew la trouve très belle. Il est à nouveau intimidé, mais il frappe à la porte.

Une jolie blonde ouvre la porte.

« **Salut**, Diana », sourit Andrew.

« **Quoi de neuf**? » dit Diana. Son pyjama est rose vif et ses cheveux sont sales.

«**Comment ça va?**» demande Andrew.

« **Ça va**, dit Diana. Je dormais. Tu m'as réveillée. »

« Je suis désolé », dit-il rapidement. Son visage est rouge. Il est très timide. « J'ai un paquet. Nous ne savons pas à qui il appartient ».

« Qu'y a-t-il dedans », demande Diana.

« Des lunettes. Ce sont des lunettes pour la lecture », dit Andrew.

« Je ne porte pas de lunettes. Ma mère n'en utilise pas. Le colis n'est pas pour nous », dit Diana.

« Ok », dit Andrew. Il fait au revoir de la main et monte les escaliers. Il y a un appartement de plus, l'appartement au troisième étage. M. Edwards vit seul dans cet appartement. Il a un gros perroquet qui sait parler. Il a aussi quatre chats et un chien. Son appartement est vieux et sombre. Andrew a peur de M. Edwards. Il sonne à la porte. Il doit savoir à qui appartient le colis.

« **Bonjour** », dit M. Edwards. Son chien vient à la porte. Le chien aide M. Edwards parce qu'il est aveugle.

« Bonjour, M. Edwards, c'est Andrew », dit Andrew. M. Edwards a les yeux fermés. Il sourit.

« **Quoi de neuf**, Andrew? » demande-t-il. « Humm, pense Andrew, peut-être que M. Edwards n'est pas effrayant. Peut-être que M. Edwards est juste un gentil vieil homme qui vit seul ».

« J'ai un paquet et je pense qu'il est pour vous », dit Andrew.

« Ah oui! Mes lunettes de lecture. Enfin!» sourit M. Edwards. Il tend les mains. Andrew est confus.

Il regarde le chien. Il semble sourire aussi. Il donne le colis à M. Edwards.

« **Je suis content de te voir**, dit M. Edwards.

« **Moi aussi** », dit Andrew. Il rendra peut-être visite à M. Edwards un autre jour. Il se retourne et rentre chez lui.

RÉSUMÉ

Un garçon, Andrew, reçoit un colis qui ne lui est pas destiné. C'est un colis qui contient des lunettes. Il l'apporte aux voisins, un par un, pour savoir à qui appartient le colis. Il découvre que le colis appartient à son voisin M. Edwards, ce qui est un peu surprenant.

Liste de Vocabulaire

Good morning	Bonjour
Hello	Bonjour
Sir	Monsieur
Thank you very much	Merci beaucoup
Bye	Bye
Morning!	Bonjour!
How are you?	Comment ça va?
Fine, thanks!	Très bien, merci!
And you?	Et vous?
Ma'am	Madame
Hi!	Salut!
My name is...	Mon nom est...
It's nice to meet you.	Ravi de vous rencontrer.

Nice to meet you too.	Ravi de vous rencontrer également.
How's it going?	Comment ça va?
It's going.	Ça va.
Hey!	Salut!
What's up?	Quoi de neuf?
What's new?	Quoi de neuf?
It's good to see you.	Je suis content de te voir.

QUESTIONS

1. Qui est à la porte d'entrée lorsqu'Andrew l'ouvre?

    a) un livreur

    b) un chat

    c) un recenseur

d) son père

2. Comment décririez-vous Mme Smith?

a) une belle fille

b) une méchante personne

c) une mauvaise voisine

d) une vieille femme gentille

3. Qui habite au deuxième étage de l'immeuble?

a) personne

b) une fille de l'école d'Andrew

c) une nouvelle famille

d) Andrew

4. A votre avis, que pense Andrew de Diana?

a) il l'aime bien et il pense qu'elle est jolie

b) il la suit sur les réseaux sociaux

c) il ne l'aime pas

d) ils ne se connaissent pas

5. À qui dans l'immeuble appartiennent les lunettes ?

a) à la vieille femme

b) à l'homme aveugle

c) à Andrew et sa famille

d) à personne

RÉPONSES

1. Qui est à la porte d'entrée lorsqu'Andrew l'ouvre?

a) un livreur

2. Comment décririez-vous Mme Smith?

    d) une vieille femme gentille

3. Qui habite au deuxième étage de l'immeuble?

    c) une nouvelle famille

4. A votre avis, que pense Andrew de Diana?

    a) il l'aime bien et pense qu'elle est jolie

5. À qui dans l'immeuble appartiennent les lunettes ?

    b) à l'homme aveugle

Translation of the Story

The Mysterious Package

The doorbell rings.

Andrew runs to the door of the apartment. The doorbell never rings on Saturday mornings. Andrew is excited to see who is at the door. He opens the door.

"**Good morning**, little boy," says a delivery man. The man is dressed in a brown uniform and is carrying a brown box.

"**Hello**, **sir**," says Andrew.

"I have a package," the delivery man says. "It says 10 Main Street."

"This is 10 Main Street," says Andrew.

"The package has no name," says the delivery man. "It also has no apartment number."

"How strange!" says Andrew.

"Can you give it to the right person?" the man asks.

"I can try," says Andrew. He is only ten years old, but he feels important.

"Thank you very much," says the delivery man. He leaves. Andrew takes the box into his house. He stares at the box. It is about the size of a shoe box. It has no name on the outside, just 10 Main Street.

Andrew opens the cardboard box. He needs to know what is inside to find the owner. There is a small wood box inside the cardboard box. Andrew opens the wooden box. Inside the box are 10 different pairs of eyeglasses. They are different colors: pink and red, green polka dots, black and white. They are also different shapes: round, square and rectangle.

He closes the box and puts on his shoes.

"**Bye** mom! I'll be right back," he shouts.

Andrew knocks on the door across the hall from his house. It opens. A very old lady smiles at Andrew and the box.

"**Morning**, Mrs. Smith!" says Andrew.

"How are you?" asks the old lady.

"Fine, thanks! And you?" says Andrew.

"What do you have?" asks the old lady.

"Ma'am, this is a package. It belongs to someone in this building but I don't know who," says Andrew.

"It's not for me," says the old lady. "Impossible!"

"Oh, ok" says Andrew, disappointed. The old lady wears glasses. He thinks these glasses would look nice on her. He turns to leave.

"Come back later," calls the old lady. "I'm making cookies and some cookies are for you and your family."

Andrew goes up the stairs. His building has three floors. He is friends with almost everyone in the building. However, the apartment on the second floor has a new family. Andrew doesn't know them. He feels shy, but he rings the bell. A brown-haired man opens the door. He smiles.

"Hi!" says the man.

"Hello," says Andrew. "I live downstairs. **My name is** Andrew."

"It's nice to meet you, Andrew," the man says. "We are new to the building. I'm Mr. Jones."

"Nice to meet you too," says Andrew. "This package belongs to someone in this building. Is it your package?"

"Impossible!" says the man. "My family and I just moved here. No one knows our address."

"Ok," says Andrew. "Nice to meet you then." The door closes. Another no. There are only two apartments left to try. In the next apartment is a family. The daughter goes to the same school as Andrew. She is a year older than Andrew. Her name is Diana. Andrew thinks she is very beautiful. He feels shy again, but he knocks on the door.

A pretty, blonde girl opens the door.

"Hey, Diana," Andrew smiles.

"What's up?" Diana says. Her pijamas are bright pink and her hair is messy.

"How's it going?" Andrew asks.

"It's going," Diana says. "I was asleep. You woke me up."

"I'm sorry," he says quickly. His face is red. He feels extra shy. "I have a package. We don't know who it belongs to."

"What is in it?" asks Diana.

"Some glasses. They are glasses for reading," says Andrew.

"I don't wear glasses. My mom doesn't use them. The box is not for us," says Diana.

"Ok," says Andrew. He waves goodbye and climbs the stairs. There is one more apartment, the apartment on the third floor. Mr. Edwards lives in this apartment, alone. He has a big parrot that knows how to talk. He also has four cats and a dog. His apartment is old and dark. Andrew feels afraid of Mr. Edwards. He rings the doorbell. He has to find out who the box belongs to.

"Hello," says Mr. Edwards. His dog comes to the door. The dog helps Mr. Edwards because he is blind.

"Hi, Mr. Edwards. It's Andrew," Andrew says. Mr. Edwards has his eyes closed. He smiles.

"What's new, Andrew?" He asks. Hmmm, Andrew thinks, maybe Mr. Edwards isn't scary. Maybe Mr. Edwards is just a nice old man that lives alone.

"I have a package and I think it is for you," says Andrew.

"Ah yes! My reading glasses. Finally!" smiles Mr. Edwards. He holds his hands out. Andrew is confused. He looks at the dog. It seems to be smiling, too. He gives Mr. Edwards the box.

"It's good to see you," says Mr. Edwards.

"You too," says Andrew. Maybe he will visit Mr. Edwards another day. He turns around and goes home.

CHAPTER 2
Mardi Gras / Colors + Days of the Week

HISTOIRE

Frank sort de chez lui. Sa nouvelle maison est **violette** avec des fenêtres **bleues**. Les **couleurs** sont très vives pour une maison. À la Nouvelle-Orléans, où est sa nouvelle maison, les bâtiments sont colorés.

Il est nouveau dans le quartier. Frank n'a pas encore d'amis. La maison à côté de chez lui est un grand bâtiment **rouge**. Une famille y vit. Frank regarde la porte, et un homme l'ouvre. Frank dit bonjour.

« Bonjour, voisin! » dit George. Il fait signe de la main. Frank marche en direction de la maison rouge.

« Bonjour, je suis Frank, le nouveau voisin », dit Frank.

« Ravi de vous rencontrer. Je m'appelle George », dit-il. Les hommes se serrent la main. George a une guirlande lumineuse dans les mains. Les lumières sont **vertes**, **violettes** et **dorées**.

« Cette guirlande lumineuse est pour quoi? » demande Frank.

« Vous êtes nouveau, » rit George. « C'est Mardi Gras, ne le saviez-vous pas ? Ces couleurs représentent la fête du carnaval ici à la Nouvelle-Orléans. »

« Oh, oui », dit Frank. Frank ne connaît pas le carnaval. Il n'a pas non plus d'amis avec qui faire des projets.

« Aujourd'hui, c'est **vendredi**, dit George. Il y a un défilé appelé Endymion. Viendrez-vous avec moi et ma famille pour le voir? »

« Oui, dit Frank. Génial! »

George mets la guirlande lumineuse sur la maison. Frank aide George. George allume la lumière. La maison semble festive.

La famille et Frank se rendent au défilé. Pendant Mardi gras à la Nouvelle-Orléans, il y a des défilés tous les jours. Les défilés pendant la **semaine** sont petits. Les défilés du week-end, **samedi** et **dimanche**, sont grands, avec beaucoup de chars et de gens. Il y a un roi du Mardi Gras. Il s'appelle Rex.

Mardi gras signifie « **mardi** gras ». En Angleterre, on l'appelle « Shrove Tuesday » (« mardi de confession »). C'est une fête catholique. C'est le jour avant le Mercredi des Cendres, le début du Carême. Mardi Gras est la célébration qui précède le Carême, un moment sérieux. Arrivé Jeudi, les jours de fête sont terminés. La Nouvelle-Orléans est célèbre pour son Mardi Gras. Les gens font des fêtes et portent des masques et des costumes. En fait, vous ne pouvez porter un masque à la Nouvelle-Orléans que pour Mardi Gras. Le reste de l'année, c'est illégal !

George et sa famille regardent le défilé qui commence avec Frank. Frank est surpris. Il y a beaucoup de gens qui regardent. Ils sont debout dans l'herbe. Les chars passent devant le groupe.

Les chars sont de grandes structures avec des gens et des décorations. Ils descendent la rue, un par un.

Le premier char représente le soleil. Il a des décorations **jaunes**. Une femme au milieu porte une robe **blanche**. Elle ressemble à un ange. Elle jette des jouets et des perles orange aux gens.

« Pourquoi jette-t-elle les jouets et les colliers? » demande Frank.

« Pour nous! » dit Hannah, la femme de George. Hannah tient cinq colliers dans ses mains. Il y a des perles sur le sol. Personne ne les attrape. Elles sont sales et **marrons**.

Le défilé se poursuit. Il y a beaucoup de chars et de perles. George et sa famille crient : « Jetez-moi quelque chose, monsieur! » Hannah remplit son sac **noir** de jouets colorés et de perles provenant des chars. Frank apprend à crier « Jetez-moi quelque chose! » pour recevoir des perles pour lui.

Un grand char compte plus de 250 personnes. C'est le plus grand char au monde.

Enfin, le défilé se termine. Les enfants et les adultes sont heureux. Tout le monde rentre chez soi. Frank est fatigué. Il a faim aussi et il veut manger. Il suit George et sa famille dans la maison **rouge**. Il y a un gros gâteau rond sur la table. Il ressemble à un anneau, avec un trou au milieu. Le gâteau est recouvert d'un glaçage **violet**, **vert** et **jaune**.

« C'est le gâteau du roi », dit Hannah. « Nous mangeons du gâteau du roi tous les mardis gras. »

Hannah coupe un morceau de gâteau. Elle en donne un à George, un autre aux enfants et un autre à Frank. Frank goûte le gâteau. Il est délicieux! Il a un goût de cannelle. Il est moelleux. Mais soudainement Frank mord dans du plastique.

« Aïe! » dit Frank. Frank arrête de manger. Il sort un bébé en plastique du gâteau.

« Il y a une autre tradition, dit George. Le gâteau contient un bébé. La personne qui reçoit le bébé achète le prochain gâteau. »

« C'est moi ! » dit Frank.

Tout le monde rit. George invite Frank à un autre défilé **lundi**.

Frank rentre chez lui heureux. Il adore Mardi Gras.

Liste de vocabulaire

violet	violet
blue	bleu
colors	couleurs
red	rouge
green	vert
purple	pourpre
gold	or
Friday	vendredi
week	semaine
Saturday	Samedi
Sunday	dimanche
Tuesday	mardi

Wednesday	mercredi
Thursday	jeudi
yellow	jaune
white	blanc
orange	orange
brown	marron
black	noir
Monday	lundi

QUESTIONS

1) Comment décririez-vous la nouvelle maison de Frank?

    a) ennuyeuse

    b) colorée

    c) minuscule

    d) isolée

2) Quelle couleur représente Mardi Gras à la Nouvelle-Orléans ?

a) bleu

b) blanc

c) orange

d) or

3) Mardi gras est une fête :

a) réservée aux adultes.

b) de la tradition de l'Église juive.

c) célèbre à la Nouvelle-Orléans.

d) que vous célébrez à l'intérieur d'une maison.

4) Laquelle de ces réponses ne se trouve pas sur un char de Mardi Gras ?

a) des gens

b) des ordinateurs

c) des jouets

d) des perles

5) Que se passe-t-il si vous trouvez le bébé dans un gâteau royal?

a) vous pleurez

b) vous devez prendre soin du bébé

c) vous le donnez à votre ami

d) vous devez acheter un gâteau roi

RÉPONSES

1) Comment décririez-vous la nouvelle maison de Frank?

b) colorée

2) Quelle couleur représente Mardi Gras à la Nouvelle-Orléans ?

    d) or

3) Mardi gras est une fête :

    c) célèbre à la Nouvelle-Orléans.

4) Laquelle de ces réponses ne se trouve pas sur un char de Mardi Gras ?

    b) des ordinateurs

5) Que se passe-t-il si vous trouvez le bébé dans un gâteau du roi?

    d) vous devez acheter un gâteau roi

Translation of the Story

Mardi Gras

STORY

Frank steps out his front door. His new house is **violet** with **blue** windows. The **colors** are very bright for a house. In New Orleans, his new home, buildings are colorful.

He is new to the neighborhood. Frank does not have any friends yet. The house next to him is a tall, **red** building. A family lives there. Frank stares at the door, and a man opens it. Frank says hello.

"Hello, neighbor!" says George. He waves. Frank walks to the red house.

"Hi, I'm Frank, the new neighbor," says Frank.

"Nice to meet you. My name is George," George says. The men shake hands. George has a string of lights in his hands. The lights are **green**, **purple** and **gold**.

"What are the lights for?" asks Frank.

"You *are* new," laughs George. "It's Mardi Gras, didn't you know? These colors represent the holiday of carnival here in New Orleans."

"Oh, yes," says Frank. Frank does not know about carnival. He also has no friends to make plans with.

"Today is **Friday**," says George. "There is a parade called Endymion. Will you come with me and the family to watch?"

"Yes," Frank says. "Wonderful!"

George puts the lights on the house. Frank helps George. George turns on the lights. The house looks festive.

The family and Frank go to the parade. During Mardi Gras in New Orleans, there are parades every day. The parades during the **week** are small. The parades on the weekend, **Saturday** and **Sunday**, are big, with many floats and people. There is a king of Mardi Gras. His name is Rex.

Mardi Gras means 'Fat **Tuesday**'. In England, it is called Shrove Tuesday. The holiday is Catholic. It is one day before Ash **Wednesday**, the beginning of Lent. Mardi Gras is the celebration before Lent, a serious time. By **Thursday**, the special days are finished. New Orleans is famous for its Mardi Gras. People have parties and wear masks and costumes. In fact, you can only wear a mask in New Orleans on Mardi Gras. The rest of the year it is illegal!

George and his family watch the parade begin with Frank. Frank is surprised. There are many people watching. They stand in the grass. Floats pass the group. Floats are big structures with people and decorations. They go down the street, one by one.

The first float represents the sun. It has **yellow** decorations. A woman in the middle wears a **white** dress. She looks like an angel. She throws **orange** toys and beads to the people.

"Why does she throw the toys and necklaces?" asks Frank.

"For us!" says Hannah, George's wife. Hannah holds five necklaces in her hands. Some beads are on the ground. Nobody catches them. They are dirty and **brown**.

The parade continues. There are many floats, and many beads. George and his family shout, "Throw me something, mister!" Hannah fills her **black** bag with colorful toys and beads from the floats. Frank learns to shout "Throw me something!" to get beads for himself.

One big float has over 250 people on it. It is the largest in the world.

Finally, the parade ends. The children and the adults are happy. Everyone goes home. Frank is tired. He is also hungry and wants to eat. He follows George and his family into the **red** house. There is a big, round cake on the table. It looks like a ring, with a hole in the middle. The cake has **purple**, **green** and **yellow** frosting on top.

"This is king cake," Hannah says. "We eat king cake every Mardi Gras."

Hannah cuts a piece of cake. She gives one piece to George, one piece to the children, and one piece to Frank. Frank tastes the cake. It is delicious! It tastes like cinnamon. It is soft. But suddenly Frank bites into plastic.

"Ouch!" says Frank. Frank stops eating. He pulls a plastic baby out of the cake.

"There is one more tradition," says George. "The cake has a baby in it. The person who gets the baby buys the next cake."

"That's me!" Frank says.

Everyone laughs. George invites Frank to another parade on **Monday.**

Frank goes home happy. He loves Mardi Gras.

CHAPTER 3
Weird Weather / Weather

HISTOIRE

Ivan est âgé de 12 ans. Il rend visite à ses grands-parents le week-end. Il adore rendre visite à ses grands-parents. Grand-mère lui donne des biscuits et du lait tous les jours. Grand-père lui apprend des choses intéressantes. Ce week-end, il va chez eux.

On est en février. Ivan est là, c'est l'**hiver**. En février, il **neige** habituellement. Ivan adore la neige. Il joue dans la neige et en fait des boules. Ce week-end de février, le **temps** est différent. Le soleil brille, il fait **beau** et il fait presque **chaud**! Ivan porte un T-shirt chez ses grands-parents.

« Bonjour, grand-père! Bonjour, grand-mère! »,
dit Ivan.

« Bonjour, Ivan! », dit Grand-mère.

« Ivan! Comment vas-tu? », dit Grand-père.

« Je vais bien », dit-il, et il embrasse ses grands-
parents. Ivan dit au revoir à sa mère.

Ils entrent dans la maison. « Ce temps est étrange,
dit Grand-mère. En février, il fait toujours **froid**
et **nuageux**. Je ne comprends pas! »

« C'est le **changement climatique** », dit Ivan.
À l'école, Ivan étudie la contamination et la
pollution. Le temps change en raison des
changements dans **l'atmosphère**. Le

changement climatique, c'est la différence de météo à travers le temps.

« Je ne suis pas au courant des changements climatiques, dit Grand-père. Je **prédis** le temps en fonction de ce que je vois. »

« Que veux-tu dire ? », demande Ivan.

« Ce matin, le **ciel** est rouge, dit Grand-père. Cela signifie que je sais qu'une **tempête** approche. »

« Comment ? » demande Ivan.

« Ciel rouge le matin avertit le marin. Ciel rouge le soir donne espoir. » Grand-père explique ce dicton à Ivan.

Si le ciel est rouge au lever du soleil, cela signifie qu'il y a de l'eau dans l'air. La lumière du soleil brille rouge. La tempête vient vers vous. Si le ciel est rouge au coucher du soleil, le mauvais temps part. Sans **présentateur météo**, les gens regardent le ciel pour chercher des indices sur le temps.

« Comment les météorologues prédisent-ils le temps? » demande Ivan.

« Ils observent les tendances dans l'atmosphère, dit Grand-mère. Ils observent la température, si elle est chaude ou froide. Et ils observent la pression atmosphérique, ce qui se passe dans l'atmosphère. »

« Je prédis les la météo différemment, dit Grand-père. Par exemple, je sais qu'il va **pleuvoir** aujourd'hui. »

« Comment ? », demande Ivan.

« Le chat », dit Grand-père. Ivan regarde le chat. Le chat ouvre la bouche et fait « ah-CHOO ».

« Quand le chat éternue ou ronfle, cela signifie qu'il va pleuvoir, dit Grand-père. Il va peut-être **bruiner** ou il peut beaucoup **pleuvoir**, mais il va y avoir de la pluie. »

Soudain, ils entendent un son fort. Ivan regarde par la fenêtre. Les gouttes de pluie tombent fort. La pluie est forte. Ivan ne peut pas entendre ce que son grand-père dit.

« Quoi? », dit Ivan.

« Il **pleut des cordes** », dit grand-père en souriant.

« Ah! » rit Ivan.

« Je connais un autre moyen de connaître la météo », dit grand-mère.

Grand-mère regarde les araignées pour voir quand il fera froid. À la fin de l'**été**, le temps change. L'**automne** apporte de l'air frais et froid. Grand-mère sait que lorsque les araignées entrent à l'intérieur, cela signifie que le froid arrive. Les araignées font une maison à l'intérieur avant l'hiver. C'est comme ça que grand-mère sait quand le temps hivernal arrive.

La pluie s'arrête. Grand-père et Ivan sortent. Grand-père et Grand-mère vivent dans une maison dans la forêt. La maison est entourée d'arbres. C'est une petite maison. Ivan a froid dans son t-shirt. Le temps n'est pas ensoleillé.

L'air se déplace. Il y a du vent. Le vent souffle dans les cheveux d'Ivan.

« Il fait **froid** maintenant », dit Ivan.

« Oui, dit grand-père. Quelle est la température? »

« Je ne sais pas, dit Ivan. Je n'ai pas de thermomètre. »

« Tu n'en as pas besoin », dit grand-père. Grand-père dit à Ivan d'écouter. Ivan entend un son : cri-cri-cri. C'est un insecte. Le cri-cri-cri est le son des grillons. Grand-père enseigne quelque chose à Ivan. Ivan compte les *cris* pendant quatorze secondes. Grand-père ajoute 40 à ce nombre. C'est la température à l'extérieur. Ivan ne savait pas que les grillons étaient comme des thermomètres.

Grand-mère sort de la maison. Elle sourit. Elle regarde Ivan compter les cricris. « C'est l'heure des biscuits et du lait! » dit-elle.

« Oui! », dit Ivan.

« Oh, regardez! » dit grand-mère. « C'est un arc-en-ciel. » L'arc-en-ciel va de la maison à la forêt. Il a plusieurs couleurs : rouge, orange, jaune, bleu et vert. L'arc-en-ciel est magnifique. Grand-mère, grand-père et Ivan regardent l'arc-en-ciel. Il disparaît et ils rentrent.

« Des biscuits et du lait pour tout le monde », dit grand-mère. Elle donne à Ivan un biscuit au chocolat encore chaud.

« Pas pour moi, dit Grand-père. Je veux du thé. »

« Pourquoi du thé? » dit Grand-mère. Elle a deux verres de lait à la main.

« Avec ce temps, je ne me sens un peu malade », dit grand-père. Il rit. Ivan et grand-mère rient avec lui.

Liste de Vocabulaire

winter	hiver
to snow	à la neige
weather	temps
sunny	ensoleillé
hot	chaud
cold	froid
cloudy	nuageux
climate change	changements climatiques

atmosphere	atmosphère
predict	prédire
sky	ciel
storm	tempête
weathermen	Présentateur météo
drizzle	bruine
rainy	pluvieux
raining cats and dogs	Il pleut des cordes
summer	été
autumn	automne
windy	venteux
temperature	température
thermometer	thermomètre
rainbow	arc-en-ciel
under the weather	pas dans son assiette

QUESTIONS

1) À quoi ressemble habituellement la météo en février?

    a) il fait chaud

    b) il fait froid

    c) il y a du soleil

    d) il fait frais

2) Comment grand-père sait-il quel temps il fera?

    a) il regarde la télévision

    b) les conditions météorologiques

    c) il observe la nature

    d) il ne prédit pas le temps

3) Qu'est-ce que signifie « tomber des cordes »?

    a) la pluie mouille les cordes

b) il pleut juste un peu

c) les chats et les chiens tombent du ciel

d) il pleut très fort

4) Qu'est-ce que cela signifie lorsque les araignées rentrent à l'intérieur?

a) elles ont faim

b) elles sont prêtes à pondre des œufs

c) le temps froid arrive

d) le temps chaud arrive

5) Pourquoi Grand-père demande-t-il du thé au lieu du lait?

a) il se sent un peu malade

b) il est allergique au lait

c) il veut une boisson chaude

d) pour mettre Grand-mère en colère

RÉPONSES

1) À quoi ressemble habituellement la météo en février?

a) il fait chaud

2) Comment grand-père sait-il quel temps il fera?

c) il observe la nature

3) Que signifie « tomber des cordes »?

d) il pleut très fort

4) Qu'est-ce que cela signifie lorsque les araignées rentrent à l'intérieur?

c) le temps froid arrive

5) Pourquoi grand-père demande-t-il du thé au lieu du lait?

a) il se sent un peu malade

Translation of the Story

Weird Weather

STORY

Ivan is twelve years old. He visits his grandparents on the weekend. He loves to visit his grandparents. Grandma gives him cookies and milk every day. Grandpa teaches him neat things. This weekend he goes to their house.

It is February. Where Ivan is, it is **winter**. In February, it usually **snows**. Ivan loves the snow. He plays in it and rolls it into balls. This February weekend, the **weather** is different. The sun is shining; it is **sunny** and almost **hot**! Ivan wears a T-shirt to his grandparent's house.

"Hi, Grandpa! Hi, Grandma!" Ivan says.

"Hello, Ivan!" Grandma says.

"Ivan! How are you?" says Grandpa.

"I'm good," he says, and he hugs his grandparents. Ivan says goodbye to his mom.

They go into the house. "This weather is strange," says Grandma. "February is always **cold** and **cloudy**. I don't understand!"

"It is **climate change**," says Ivan. In school, Ivan learns about contamination and pollution. The weather changes because of changes in the **atmosphere**. Climate change is the difference in the weather over time.

"I don't know about climate change," says Grandpa. "I **predict** the weather by what I see."

"What do you mean?" asks Ivan.

"This morning, the **sky** is red," says Grandpa. "This means I know a **storm** is coming."

"How?" asks Ivan.

"Red sky in the morning, sailors take warning. Red sky at night, sailor's delight." Grandpa tells Ivan about this saying.

If the sky is red at sunrise, it means there is water in the air. The light of the sun shines red. The storm is coming towards you. If the sky is red at sunset, the bad weather is leaving. Without **weathermen**, people watch the sky for clues about the weather.

"How do weathermen predict the weather?" asks Ivan.

"They look at patterns in the atmosphere," says Grandma. "They look at temperature, if it is hot or cold. And they look at air pressure, what is happening in the atmosphere."

"I predict the weather differently," says Grandpa. "For example, I know today it will **rain**."

"How?" asks Ivan.

"The cat," says Grandpa. Ivan looks at the cat. The cat opens its mouth and says 'ah-CHOO'.

"When the cat sneezes or snores, that means rain is coming," says Grandpa. It may **drizzle** or it may be very **rainy**, but it will rain."

Suddenly, they hear a loud sound. Ivan looks out the window. Drops of rain are falling hard. The rain is loud. Ivan can't hear what his Grandpa says.

"What?" says Ivan.

"It's **raining cats and dogs**," says Grandpa, smiling.

"Ha!" laughs Ivan.

"I know another way to tell the weather," says Grandma.

Grandma watches the spiders to see when the weather will be cold. At the end of **summer**, the weather changes. **Autumn** brings fresh, cool air. Grandma knows that when spiders come inside, it means cold weather is coming. The spiders make

79

a house inside before winter. That is how grandma knows when the winter weather comes.

The rain stops. Grandpa and Ivan go out. Grandpa and Grandma live in a house in the forest. The house has trees around it. It is a small house. Ivan is cold in his T-shirt. The weather is not sunny. The air is moving. It is **windy**. The wind blows through Ivan's hair.

"It is **cold** now," says Ivan.

"Yes," says Grandpa. "What is the temperature?"

"I don't know," says Ivan. "I don't have a thermometer."

"You don't need one," says Grandpa. Grandpa tells Ivan to listen. Ivan hears a sound: *cri-cri-cri.* It is an insect. The *cri-cri-cri* is the sound of crickets. Grandpa teaches Ivan. Ivan counts the *cri* for fourteen seconds. Grandpa adds 40 to that number. That is the temperature outside. Ivan did not know crickets were like thermometers.

Grandma comes out of the house. She smiles. She watches Ivan counting the *cri* sound. "Time for cookies and milk!" she says.

"Yay!" says Ivan.

"Oh, look!" says Grandma. "It's a rainbow." The rainbow goes from the house to the forest. It has many colors: red, orange, yellow, blue and green. The rainbow is beautiful. Grandma, Grandpa and Ivan watch the rainbow. It disappears and they go inside.

"Cookies and milk for everyone," says Grandma. She gives Ivan a warm chocolate cookie.

"Not for me," says Grandpa. "I want tea."

"Why tea?" says Grandma. She has two milks in her hand.

"I'm feeling **under the weather**," says Grandpa. He laughs. Ivan and Grandma laugh with him.

CONCLUSION

Y ou did it!

You finished a whole book in a brand-new language. That in and of itself is quite the accomplishment, isn't it?

Congratulate yourself on time well spent and a job well done. Now that you've finished the book, you have familiarized yourself with over 500 new vocabulary words, comprehended the heart of 3 short stories, and listened to loads of dialogue unfold, all without going anywhere!

Charlemagne said "To have another language is to possess a second soul." After immersing yourself in this book, you are broadening your horizons and opening a whole new path for yourself.

Have you thought about how much you know now that you did not know before? You've learned everything from how to greet and how to express your emotions to basics like colors and place words. You can tell time and ask question. All without opening a schoolbook. Instead, you've cruised through fun, interesting stories and possibly listened to them as well.

Perhaps before you weren't able to distinguish meaning when you listened to French. If you used the audiobook, we bet you can now pick out meanings and words when you hear someone speaking. Regardless, we are sure you have taken an important step to being more fluent. You are well on your way!

Best of all, you have made the essential step of distinguishing in your mind the idea that most often hinders people studying a new language. By approaching French through our short stories and dialogs, instead of formal lessons with just grammar and vocabulary, you are no longer in the 'learning' mindset. Your approach is much more similar to an osmosis, focused on speaking and using the language, which is the end goal, after all!

So, what's next?

This is just the first of five books, all packed full of short stories and dialogs, covering essential, everyday French that will ensure you master the basics. You can find the rest of the books in the series, as well as a whole host of other resources, at LearnLikeNatives.com. Simply add the book to your library to take the next step in your language learning journey. If you are ever in need of new ideas or direction, refer to our 'Speak Like a Native' eBook, available to you for free at LearnLikeNatives.com, which clearly outlines practical steps you can take to continue learning any language you choose.

We also encourage you to get out into the real world and practice your French. You have a leg up on most beginners, after all—instead of pure textbook learning, you have been absorbing the sound and soul of the language. Do not underestimate the foundation you have built reviewing the chapters of this book. Remember, no one feels 100% confident when they speak with a native speaker in another language.

One of the coolest things about being human is connecting with others. Communicating with someone in their own language is a wonderful gift. Knowing the language turns you into a local and opens up your world. You will see the reward of learning languages for many years to come, so keep that practice up!. Don't let your fears stop you from taking the chance to use your French.

Just give it a try, and remember that you will make mistakes. However, these mistakes will teach you so much, so view every single one as a small victory! Learning is growth.

Don't let the quest for learning end here! There is so much you can do to continue the learning process in an organic way, like you did with this book. Add another book from Learn Like a Native to your library. Listen to French talk radio. Watch some of the great French films. Put on the latest CD from Edith Piaf. Take cooking lessons in French. Whatever you do, don't stop because every little step you take counts towards learning a new language, culture, and way of communicating.

www.LearnLikeNatives.com

Learn Like a Native is a revolutionary **language education brand** that is taking the linguistic world by storm. Forget boring grammar books that never get you anywhere, Learn Like a Native teaches you languages in a fast and fun way that actually works!

As an international, multichannel, language learning platform, we provide **books, audio guides and eBooks** so that you can acquire the knowledge you need, swiftly and easily.

Our **subject-based learning**, structured around real-world scenarios, builds your conversational muscle and ensures you learn the content most relevant to your requirements. Discover our tools at *LearnLikeNatives.com*.

When it comes to learning languages, we've got you covered!

Printed in Great Britain
by Amazon

41930127R00050